Advance Praise for *The Naked Room*

Are you curious to visit the darkest corners of rooms on the edges of the spectrum of humanity? Do you want a peek inside the asylums and the minds of these asylums' inhabitants? Willa Schneberg's *Naked Room*, a mix of persona poems, found poetry and personal narrative, takes us on an international tour of the dysregulated.

Although the journey through *The Naked Room* may be frightening at times, in the hands of this masterful poet and her beautiful visceral language, the journey is somehow magnificent.

> —Leanne Grabel, author of *Brontosaurus Illustrated* & *My Husband's Eyebrows*

In this welcome book of poems psyche bursts into words, Life bursts into words. Do we care for Life, does Life care for us? Feelings from many levels of being have their say and open cracks and nuances of who and what we are. At once a celebration, exploration and a caution about our precious gift of experience.

> —Michael Eigen, Ph.D., author of *The Challenge of Being Human*, *The Sensitive Self* & *The Psychoanalytic Mystic*

These staggering poems, written in direct, potent language, cast an eye over the history of psychological care—hundreds of years. Brave, moving, virtuosic, and unflinching words that will stick with you.

> —Shawn Levy, author of *A Year in the Life of Death*, *The Castle on Sunset*, & *In on the Joke*

Also by Willa Schneberg

Box Poems
In The Margins Of TheWorld
Storytelling in Cambodia
The Books of Esther
Rending The Garment

THE NAKED ROOM

POEMS

WILLA SCHNEBERG

Broadstone

Text & Cover Design by Larry W. Moore
Cover photograph, "Cremains Memorial, Oregon State Hospital"
by the author

Broadstone Books
An Imprint of
Broadstone Media LLC
418 Ann Street
Frankfort, KY 40601-1929
BroadstoneBooks.com

To my life partner, Robin Bagai, who believed in this collection
before I could, who has been known to say,
Go deeper, equanimity is not the goal.

To Nancy Gurian, who always believed
this manuscript would find a home.

CONTENTS

ASYLUM

Yellow Halo / 3

Unsanctioned / 4

The Majesty of Mania / 5

Admission Criteria For Oregon State Insane Asylum, 1906 / 7

Tiny Monuments / 8

Intake At The Canton Asylum For Insane Indians / 9

From The Chart Of Yanna Nommik / 10

The Marines Came Through The Gates / 12

Deinstitutionalization / 13

CASE HISTORY

Iron Lung / 17

American History / 18

Life Line / 19

Ugly / 20

Vapor / 21

There Are Countries / 22

Prayer Of A Sleep Eater / 23

Sleeping Beauty / 24

How to Set The Table / 25

The Bodies Are Messages / 26

Virtual / 27

Song Of A Rental Sister / 28

She Feeds Me Mangoes / 30

STRAITJACKET

"I" / 33

The Tub Seduction / 34

Exposure, 1856 / 35

Like Coring An Apple / 37

She Was A Kennedy / 39

Love / 41
Black Box / 42
Dr. Henry Anonymous Speaks At The 1972 APA Convention / 43
Prayer Of A Pedophile / 44
Nightmare, Recurrent / 45
SIM Card Seller / 46
Skin / 47

FIFTY-MINUTE HOUR

Pearls / 51
The First Therapist / 52
Wind Freezes Trees In Tortured Positions / 53
The Unspoken / 54
Interviewing A New Therapist / 56
Confidentiality / 57
To Inhabit The Body / 59
Couple Counseling / 60
Dream Session, CLIENT I / 61
Dream Session, CLIENT II / 62

REALITY TESTING

Tasters / 65
Prayer Of An Apotemnophile / 66
Missing Person / 67
Now I Don't Ask / 68
Psychosis / 69
Florid / 70
72" x 72" / 72
Her Rorschach / 73

TERMINATION

Moving / 77
Toxic / 78
Hug-A-Thug / 79

Again, I'm Going Through Rooms / 80
Moonlight / 81
Paying Homage / 82
Suicide Forest / 83
Facing Suicide Bridge / 84
In The Snooker Room / 85
Italian Plums /86
Shelley's Heart / 87

NOTES / 89

ACKNOWLEDGMENTS / 91

ABOUT THE AUTHOR / 93

To fight aloud is very brave -
But gallanter, *I know,*
Who charge within the bosom,
The Cavalry of Wo -

From "To fight aloud is very brave," Emily Dickinson

ASYLUM

Yellow Halo

Bloomingdale Asylum, New York, 1846

I plead, and they answer crooked, especially
Superintendent Pliny Earle. I birth curiosities so unique
and wondrous that they belong in the Peale Museum
next to fossilized mastodon teeth and the prong-horned antelope.

One at a time in my mind I hold a marvel just so,
until it emerges through a slit in my back that opens
and closes and disappears when God whispers.

Conical shells, nails, shank bones, horseshoes, passbooks
from Nick Biddle's bank, brass door knobs
slide out, and wasps exit and circle
above my head. They are my halo,

wear yellow jackets and are tender.
Although free to roam they choose to dwell
in this cell with me, and no longer
habit their hate-sting.

Against the attendants they are my shield,
whose voices are thunder, fingers lightning bolts
forged to strike my forceps-marked face.

Unsanctioned

Like any grand manor's garden this institution has a topiary—
kangaroos, elephants and turtles, but we are the real animals,
jezebels, segregated from male patients.

Dr. Gray calls himself "Our Protector."

In this bucolic setting, safe from noxious vapors
we are instructed to dance virtuously, recite
poems that will not excite, and become ladies again,
as if we ever were.

Tourists picnic on the manicured grounds to stare,
feel self-righteous, leave contented, and certain
that we aren't contagious.

We hide scraps of purloined butcher paper
and writing implements in our corsets,
limn depravity, and godlessness on rags
inside our thighs and behind mirrors.

We are the women relieved
our children are born dead.

In the wards at night, if we pace or scream,
we are tied to our beds, and matrons shut
our mouths with their palms until we blubber.

If Dr. Gray's minions could, they would tat
scalloped edges around our death wishes,
turn them into doilies, but sometimes
our unsanctioned words have wings:

with pieces of chalk and pencil nubs
we scratch green and yellow hot air balloons
that lift us over the padlocks.

THE MAJESTY OF MANIA
for Clifford Whittingham Beers

Refusing to part with his corncobs   he socks an attendant
        No longer docile and vegetative
                now elated and grandiose
                    he is going to gilt them   add small thermometers
                        believing once his genius is recognized
                            they will become collectibles
        Choked into submission
        he is sent to the refractory ward

The cell is six feet wide and high
windows screened and barred
the air sour   a bed screwed to the floor
coarse throw rugs

        He wants more   more debate   more books
                more pencils   more paper   more chicken pudding   more devil's
                          food cake
all denied him

In his unheated room he wears only drawers   His frozen hands cause more suffering
than the gurgling in his belly   But his mind knows that outside
        leaves turn amber and crimson, and walls hold the mutinous words he
                scratches
                        with a shiver of hidden glass

He tears the carpets into long strips
        and weaves them into a suit of rags a hermit monk might wear
                They cut him out of it   With the majesty of mania
                    he attaches straps to the foot and head of the bed
                        to the transom and the window guard

                      to make the perfect
                      adjustment   so that the bed
                        with him in it

                dangles in the air

timeless
besting Newton

Until the bullies barge in

to bludgeon him

he defies gravity

ADMISSION CRITERIA FOR OREGON STATE INSANE ASYLUM, 1906

Found Poem—from Oregon State Hospital Museum's Display Board

Brain Softening
Childbed fever
Christian Science
Disappointment in Love
General Debility
Idiocy
Lead Poisoning
Masturbation
Menopause
Nervous Prostration
Overstudy
Puerperal Trouble
Removal of Ovaries
Spiritualism
Suppressed eruption
Tobacco
Worry

Tiny Monuments

for David Maisel, who photographed canisters holding the ashes of mental patients at Oregon State Hospital.

When human beings were still locked away
for sadness clinging like a marine layer,
    voices saying how awful they are,
    going fetal when cars backfire or corks pop,
they were housed at the Oregon State Insane Asylum,
and when they ceased to be, they were cremated.

If no one claimed a brother, a daughter, or a father,
the ashes were kept in numbered copper canisters,
on pine shelves in an underground vault.

Not infrequently the water table rose,
giving the forgotten
    homes uniquely their own
coated with efflorescence and mineral dazzle,
where an alchemy of copper and water bloomed
and burst into color.

These tiny monuments to the scorned and unknown,
wear patinas of pink, burnt sienna, ocher, aqua,
    and if you look closely you will find
moon craters, archipelagos, frozen waterfalls,
Big Dippers and dunes with lone tracks.

Intake At The Canton Asylum for Insane Indians
South Dakota, 1905

Cross your legs.
Legs remain tight against each other.

Squeeze my hand.
Hand stays limp in the lap.

What is this? (Bucket)
or this? (Carrot)
The brow furrows.

1, 2, 3, 4, 5, 6, 7, 8, 9, 10
Count backwards.
Pick a favorite number.
Something hoarse whimpers out.
Perhaps charge's native tongue?

Do you feel all right, excited or depressed?
Eyes close, head flops down.

Of course, the patient speaks English,
but refuses to do so.

Done. Return to your ward.

    ***

It doesn't really matter what it is:
Creek, Apache or Sioux.
She's just another imbecile.

If you kill the Indian,
you save the man.

From The Chart of Yanna Nommik

March 3, 1946
Patient refused to lie down. Would not speak our language. Made a kissing sound. Said, Yanna, Yanna, Yanna. Would not allow an examination. This psychiatrist's face was scratched.

April 15, 1946
Patient in fetal position, blanket over the head. Pried open each fist found bread crumbs— physical health fair. Screamed unintelligible words until we left ward.

June 21, 1946
Patient on bench in courtyard head in hands until dinner hour. Refuses to engage in milieu therapy.

October 8, 1946
During rounds, patient splayed legs in a sexual manner; laughed sardonically. Gardening gloves and file cards written in a tiny script, perhaps Finnish (?) removed from pillowcase. Hospital gown revealed myriad tears.

November 15, 1947
Patient found staring out a window in corridor #2. Reportedly, she smiled at an orderly, tongue protruding between front teeth gap.

May 29, 1948
She filched a ballpoint again; wrote on hospital gown, arms, face, legs, walls and toilet seats in big loopy letters, until restrained.

August 12, 1950
Patient's hospital gown appears threadbare. When this psychiatrist tried removing it, patient spat at him, did accept a bathrobe over her shoulders; has taken to sleeping under the bed or in a utility closet; extricated daily.

October 16, 1952
Patient tried to get the male dentist's attention by baring her teeth, grinning lasciviously. Does not require dental work.

Nov. 2, 1954

Patient tapped fingers on lower teeth. We believe she wants extraction from dentist with whom she has become obsessed. Healthy teeth will not be pulled.

Feb 14, 1955

Patient pilfered a hammer, fractured jaw. Face swollen, mouth bleeding, teeth damaged and loose. Preoccupations will not be permitted. The dentist on-call, a female, will provide treatment.

THE MARINES CAME THROUGH THE GATES

Al-Rashad Psychiatric Hospital, Baghdad, May 2003

knocked down the walls
with their tanks   I can go far away now
Hannah tried   but a bullet
struck her forehead

Ahmed is somewhere   carrying a butcher knife
He said when free
he'll kill his sister

Saleem was here even longer than me
He drowned his small son and daughter
in the bathtub   On meds he forgets   Now he wants to finish the job
with the one who grew up
Maybe he's walking to him

Looters took everything: our beds bedding meds basins cookers lamps
even the frame surrounding my wife
and stomped on her
Where will I go?
She doesn't want to look at me after what I did
The world hates me
and I hate the world
I don't want to see
the monkey

DEINSTITUTIONALIZATION

Like everybody else   I want my own place
                                        Tired living
                with crazy people and the yelling
                        Plug my ears with my fingers to try to
                        block out nasty noise
                                        mean voices still won't let me be   even in this SRO
                        where nobody's here but me

        Lot of flies around here: Frosty Fudge Metamucil

Piles of doody   It stinks   The flies don't mind
Someone must of shit on the floor
                They used to serve me my meds before
                                        Once
                they showed me how to put them in little plastic cages
                but my pills want to be free like me

                        I asked for the right to fail

                        I like my filly apron although cooking hates me
                        Lost the can opener for Heinz Beans

                                Eggs are my favorite They're good soft or hard
                        A brown can dance in boiling water

                        Some pink pills escape under my pillow   some kiss ants
                in the sugar bowl   I should get me a mortar and pestle
        My grandma had one of them

                The pilot light stops working again   Frosty buzzes:
                        light a match   you won't explode
                        you'll burn up all tinselly and glitter

                                        Find a matchbook   Flames lick my frilly
                                        They won't coil me
                                                I wear my glass suit

CASE HISTORY

Iron Lung

If he could stand up he'd look like a spaceman in comics,
his head sticking out a porthole,

but my husband, who never spent a night not holding me,
except when he was deployed, cannot, he's stricken.

He puckers his lips to kiss me. I bend over, my lips barely
graze his. I want to coat his face with wet kisses,
not in front of the other wives, or their men
each in his own metal tank.

Dr. Salk's vaccine talk means nothing. Will the only
man I ever loved be able to ravish me?

When I give Sadie the robin's egg blue blanket
with the frayed satin trim and her stuffed mohair deer,
the crying stops, but during some visits so deep in myself,
her fussing doesn't register.

Everyone tries to comfort me: *He will breathe on his own*,
but not, *he'll walk again*. I won't leave his side.

Attendants pull me and the other bereft brides off
our broken men. Nurses force us to walk
back to apartments with shiny appliances
that give no comfort.

I'm expecting. Sadie rubs my tummy
and pleads, *No baby... puppy*.

AMERICAN HISTORY

Dr. Thind made history fighting to be Aryan. He was also my husband's godfather. Thind and his wife watched Robin, at four, while his mother was in labor; soon his sister's head would crest between her legs.

United States v. Bhagat Singh Thind went all the way to the Supreme Court. The justices agreed that although Thind was technically a member of the Caucasian race, he was not "Caucasian" in the popular sense of the word, so thus deemed "not white."

His citizenship was immediately revoked, and it became un-American for all South Asians, including Robin's grandfather, Vaishno Das Bagai, to be naturalized or categorized as a "free white person."

Vaishno's right to carry an American passport or own Bagai's Bazaar on Fillmore, which he had scrimped to establish, was dissolved like words on a wet piece of paper, and his reason to wear a three-piece suit, obliterated.

He booked a room in San Jose and wrote to his wife Kala, *Well dear, I have to leave you*, and turned on the gas.

I was raised with the phrase: "No Negroes, Jews or dogs allowed," warning me that I shouldn't get too comfortable. Robin and I are comfortable together. Our hands often find the other, and when we sleep at night, we spoon.

LIFE LINE

Anne Sexton addresses Maxine Kumin

We are never really disconnected,
our receivers rest on their sides
in the ready; our secret black rotary phones
are resplendent on our writing desks.

I imagine a curly black cord,
arching over your house and mine.
I just have to whistle to hear your voice,
eager to listen to what I've scribbled

after raiding rhyming dictionaries, and furiously
writing image after image of how I cycle— drown,
float face down, burst through scum,
surface, and subsist underwater.

Since your ear is right here,
I can drag a rag over baseboards, and
not smack Linda for being my little boulder
who blocks me from my drafts.

I love you, Max, without rivalry,
as I should love my sisters.
You take me far away from dribbling baby food
into a sky of words strutting.

Your voice holds me, heart sister,
whenever my critic is a harsh hammer,
with nails stuck that won't go in
and won't pry loose—
when typewriter keys say, *No!*

UGLY

It is a personal matter for the first and second wife to resolve.

Khieu Thavika—Cambodian government spokesman

I was beautiful too
and gave him sons.
I would sit in his lap
as he fastened gold
bracelets to my wrists.
He took me to Singapore.
There used to be caresses
before he entered me.
My husband is a powerful man,
high up in the government.
Powerful men don't grow old,
like their wives.

He won't replace me
with a bar girl
who sold cigarettes
and bottles of petrol on the roadside.
I will pour a vial of acid
over her head, and then a second
vial, and a third...
He will no longer want her.
She will burn and scream.
I won't stop
until she's
ugly.

VAPOR

Marcy Borders, 1973 — 2015

Knocked down on all fours, she whimpers,
I don't want to die. A photographer captures
her as she stumbles to her feet.

Coated in grey white soot, her black arms and hands
look like white evening gloves; she wears a white mustache,
a white bar across the bowl of her nose,
her nostrils are caked.

The day of dust hangs her by a noose,
although a box is never kicked from underneath,
she cannot flee, sure that Bin Laden will find her.

Smoking crack in her apartment in Bayonne
bodies are in one piece,
not fragments the size of pinkie nails,
or powder or vapor.

There Are Countries

The bones speak to us.
Sofia Egaña, forensic anthropologist

ones we live in   ones we do not
where dismembered skeletons
on stainless steel trays
will bring justice

They howl   how   the machete
the machine gun
the hammer   extinguish

Even dousing with lime & burning them
the interred bones   hold   how we hate
and won't   be silenced

PRAYER OF A SLEEP EATER

You want to walk into a dream
towards a tree bursting with apples,
pick the ripest one, crisp and green—
crunch—juice running down your chin,
and when you get up to pee
in the middle of the night
you're not rummaging
in cupboards looking for food,
eyes open and glassy,

and the next morning,
the kitchen you put to bed
is just as you left it—
no counters strewn with a mash
of chick peas and refried beans,
defrosted chicken wings, bites taken out,
peanut butter jars unlidded with craters
where your thumbs dug in,

and for once when you stick your pointer
fingers in each ear there is no stickiness,
your face is not smeared or crusty—
your hands are clean.

SLEEPING BEAUTY

In the basement where you now hide
a peck on the cheek will not rouse you.

You imagine others pricked by sorrow
slumbering too, each in her own bed with blinds drawn,
frost on their eyebrows.

Above you toilets flush yellow,
tea kettles whistle,
daffodils happily wither in jelly jars.
It seems only your windows have bars.

How To Set the Table

Forks must be on the left, knives on the right, their blades facing inward. Salad forks of course, belong left of meat forks. Spoons next to knives, away from plates; wine glasses just above the blade of the knife. If more than one wine is served glasses should be in a triangular pattern, the one on the right utilized first. Once the meal is in progress napkins must remain on laps unless in use.

I seem to be the only one who discerns there is a wrong way and a right way. The waiter doesn't appear to apprehend that either. The fool places the fork and the knife together on the left side of our dinner plates.

My breath is rapid, sweat circles spread under my arms. I feel faint and nauseous. Conversation sounds like gibberish. People look ugly and bloated. I excuse myself, lock myself in the restroom, try to heave. I must regain control.

Slowly and purposefully, I walk back to the table. When I rescue the knives, plant them to the right of our plates, (my wife is used to this, she gives me that look out of the corner of her eye), our amiable buzz resumes, and candlelight glints off the glass goblets.

THE BODIES ARE MESSAGES

Found poem from statement by Victor Hugo Ornelas,
a Mexican journalist who covers drug gangs in Guadalajara.

If it's missing a finger, it means you pointed to somebody.
Missing legs means you changed groups.
A hand cut off means it was a thief.
Missing the tongue means you said something
you shouldn't have.

VIRTUAL

You thought you liked everything unreal,
wished to live inside your computer, a chip
off your dad's block, the two of you cartwheeling
in cyberspace. Only dolts wait at check-out lines,
while you are already there.

You believed jerks watch movies in theaters,
touch elbows with smelly strangers, write with pens
on sheets of paper that fit into envelopes
needing postage, and are too lame to know,
"You got mail," and that your dad was way cool,

until he started gulping pills like candy
for his frozen shoulder. Your sister
always gave him attitude. You
leave the room when they get into it,
but the last time your dad's eyes glazed over
he wouldn't stop slugging.

Your oldest brother pulled him off her
as you hid in the closet, your dad yelling
get out, you're no children of mine.
That was all too real.

Your hatred for him doesn't disappear
like photos on Snapchat, and
you still live under the same roof.
Even before the fists, your dad could really talk
only hardware and software.

You know he thinks you're too soft, but
your sneaker collection saves you,
gives you a body. You lace up
your Nike SB Stefan Janoski Mid Zebra Pack,
and fly on your skateboard
away from the man you once adored.

Song of a Rental Sister

Why would anyone not leave his room for years?

I never tell boys I like them, but this is a job.
Their parents pay me to like them. I'm not a
prostitute or anything like that. I don't want
these boys to see me as pretty either, but as
an older sister who wears comfortable shoes.

I start with a handwritten letter on pink paper:
> *What do you do all day in your room?*
> *What's your favorite color?*
> *Do you like cats?*

If they don't respond, they are troubled, you know,
I don't give up, next time I try baby blue stationery:
> *Don't you miss walking on Takeshita Street,*
> *or slurping noodles in a noodle shop?*

and envelopes with sealing stickers
with inspirational sayings:
> *You are Awesome!*
> *Believe in Yourself!*

Boys who answer me get so personal and
confide things they would never tell their
parents, like they got beat up for having high
voices, or that they didn't try out for
anything, couldn't face not being picked; how
they peek through shutters and hate seeing
"the suits," return from work.

They text me:
> *My room is a cave, I sleep all day, leave my food tray*
> *outside my bedroom door; my avatar is decisive,*
> *a company man; I want to be "Violence Jack,"*
> *destroy evil people; I want to break my brother's ribs.*

We have a saying: A protruding nail is
hammered down. My boys are protruding
nails.

If a correspondence gets going, I move into
the delivery stage, slip pink, blue, yellow, and
if I have inspiration, purple envelopes,
beneath their bedroom doors, and wait.

Will they pry themselves from behind desk-
top computers, pick up their paper lifelines
off the floor?

If I'm really persistent and lucky, one will call
me, "Sister" through a closed door, then
inch it open.

SHE FEEDS ME MANGOES

The fact that my eyes don't work
doesn't mean that I can't see you
staring at me and my girl
with our white metal sticks
and little balls on the tips,
like unspongy marshmallows.

I guess we have to share this bus shelter.

You think, he's black and fat,
she's thin and white, and
is only with him because
she's blind.

Me and my girl love the smell of gasoline,
coconut soap, and one voice belting a cappella.

After we get home, I'll nuzzle my face
in her long luscious hair
that almost touches her ass,
she'll rest her head on my soft belly,
feed me slices of sweet tart mango.
I'll place plump fleshy cherries on her tongue,
and in my cupped hands she'll spit
the pits.

STRAITJACKET

"I"

Conjoined twins, Chang and Eng, were exhibited as curiosities. They were the 19th century's most studied human beings.

When I first felt the moist soil
of our Mount Airy farm
between my fingers
on the hand that reaches out to the world,
free of my brother's body, only then,
did I understand that Chang,
who stinks of rum,
is not me.

When I must reside
at the other house,
Chang's wife's home,
I go in body only and recite to myself
my dear Thomas Hardy:
> *Jewels in joy designed...*
> *Lie lightless, all their sparkles bleared and black and blind.*

While Adelaide, more active than women
with singletons need be, rides Chang,
I think of our cows, their udders turgid
until farmhands relieve them, and milk
squirts into tin pails.

Here, where dead leaves birth humus,
and on my porch raindrops pool,
grace would be to sit by myself
in a closed room upon a chair built for one.

The Tub Seduction

In 1908, Dr. Charles Pilgrim instituted "Tub Therapy"
at the Hudson River State Hospital.

My porcelain gleams,
bath water stays perfectly
warm and soothing. You'll recline
on a canvass hammock and lay
your head on a rubber pillow.

Don't be afraid.
I'm just like your auntie
who sucks on hard candy.
Don't worry, my lovely
you won't suck down the drain.
Dr. Pilgrim has thought of everything.

～

Time for your watery bed.
You embarrassed your spouse again,
coming to that dinner party without your blouse,
foolishly giving away your ruby necklace to the maid.

Proper will soak in. You'll repose
in my enamel crib until you are pliant,
cheerful and prune-like.

Hours and days will dissolve—
biscuits and tea, fish sticks and cranberry juice,
meatloaf and mineral water will float into your mouth.

Thank you for lending me your corporeality,
your blush, your legs, your buttocks, your back
and the nape of your neck.
You keep me hard.

Exposure, 1856

I

After a Royal Society lecture by psychiatrist John Conolly

Gentlemen, although photography is still in its infancy, we now have a superb tool to capture the characteristics of mental aberration objectively, truthfully, without the artist's subjective rendering, so evident in the paintings of poor unfortunates.

Please draw your attention to the engraving in plate 1 of an inmate afflicted with religious melancholia. This excellent product is one of Dr. Hugh Diamond's photographs. The patient's delusion is that the Great Creator has forsaken her, and that no piety or self-abnegation will provide redemption.

Please look closely. See how the camera captures what words can only approximate— the face of despair. The agonized one "knows" green pastures will not be her final resting place. Notice the wide forehead indicative of intelligence and imagination, the deep orbed eyes, the head tilted to the side unable to right itself, held up by the palm. Before the malady made the subject ashamed of her womanly body, gaiety was evident in the sunken cheeks. This calotype truly reveals the shuddering soul.

When the subject spoke, if she chose to at all, she looked down, lips barely moving as she verbalized the wish to mortify her flesh or be impaled.

Dear colleagues, as you all know, we are not always successful curing "soul sickness," psychiatry is a new science, but to our surprise and delight needlepoint stitching and industry in our modern laundry improved her condition and hastened her discharge.

II

A Former Inmate Speaks

Led in, I was instructed to sit across from a wooden box with a brass tube and told that my picture would be taken. When I protested that I didn't have proper clothing or a bonnet, the Superintendent assured me I was helping Science, and that a second photograph would be taken before I leave revealing my restored state.

I sat in a hard-backed chair, my elbow on a small side table, rested my head on my hand, my eyes focusing on happier days. I was told not to move. He would have preferred if I were a cadaver. For twenty seconds, during what he called "the exposure" I was not to smile. Did he intuit that all I wanted was the grave?

When abandoning me there, my father clasped a heavy cross around my neck. I had feared the flickering candle before he came into my bed at night, while my mother, sisters and brothers were asleep in their small deaths.

I had brought my Bible with the cracked spine, kneeled until exhausted, stretched my arms out as far as they would reach, no angel caressed my cheek.

Only in the laundry room in the company of other discarded women, did I feel my elbows and knees, and not see my body decomposing in a fiery sulfur pit. The washing tub, the scrub brush and the mangle, were my pride. When I turned the handle, wet sheets squeezed through, pressed and dried, smelling of mercy.

Finally redeemed; I buried that cross, my choker, deep inside a basket of soiled garments and walked out wearing the bonnet with purple florets I embroidered myself.

Like Coring an Apple

Just think of the brain as an apple on a wooden board,
the tip of a paring knife gently poking the top,
then push the blade all the way in
around the core, remove the knife,
and pry the core out with your thumbs.

The organ is brought up from the morgue.
Dr. Moniz, my superior, instructs me,
but it was I who performs the operation,
inserts the pen in the centrum ovale
until we are satisfied
that the depth and angle are correct
and can be replicated.

Our first living brain is easy to come by.
The brain's container and its frontal lobe
are housed in the head of a sixty-three-year-old
involutional melancholic with an auditory hallucination
demanding she poison herself with arsenic.

> Notes from Bombarda Asylum:
> Questionable sexual behavior—
> Men invited into her room for money.

Although revolutionary, our procedure is simple:
Shave hair, cleanse scalp with alcohol,
inject Novocaine, and adrenaline,
trepan holes on both sides—
all in an hour cut in half.

We interview the patient five hours later:
recalls she hailed from Calçada do Desterro,
does not know she is hospitalized;

responds to "how many fingers"
correctly with hesitation; unable
to give specific age, believes she is old.

Transferred back to Bombarda.

Final evaluation:
More docile. Patient moans and cries
with less frequency,
sans fervor or shrillness.

SHE WAS A KENNEDY

Rosemary writes to her father, October 19, 1938, London

Daddy you know I'll do anything
      to please you all tho I'm the oldest girl
I'll never be as smart as Joe, Jack
Eunic or Kit But the repoters said
In my white gown when I was presented
To the Queen I was more beautiful.
     I hate the War & the Germans.
     If it wasn't for Them I would still be
         an Assitant teacher reading & singing
     with the adorable little ones.
I would still be at Asumption with Mother Isabel and all
     the nuns who loved Me so much.

Her father talks to himself

Eighty have been treated surgically already. I respect Dr. Freeman,
who says she would be less impulsive and misbehaved,
and would no longer do something indecorous
that might derail her brothers' careers.

He described the procedure to me in great detail,
knowing I can't bear to watch, or contemplate
if unsuccessful, that my beautiful, trusting daughter
could possibly become even more impaired,
not merely *slow*, but an imbecile without language.

There will be no sedation, so each cut can be monitored.
What I don't want to imagine is that she won't
welcome having her glossy hair shaved, her hands
and feet strapped to a table, her terror
and hyperventilating as a burr hole
is trepanned into her skull.

He assures me there is some levity.
Patients are told to sing.
My Rosemary will comply,
and belt out her favorite tunes:

"You Are My Sunshine,"
"When You Wish Upon a Star."

Letter to her father, May 5, 1940, Washington, D.C.

Daddy you know I'll do whatever will make you happy.
    Do you think this surgrey will make me
Less impatient and more smarter? I hate
        St Gertrude the nuns are so mean
            I just have to yell at them sometimes.
Its like a prison   You know I am 22. Sometimes I run out
of their late at night. The City is quiet   I like hearing the clicking of my heals
        against the sidewalk. Boys talk to me.
            I know you worry about me and boys.
                    Don't worry Daddy, the Nuns always find me
                                        and tuck me in

LOVE

a straitjacket speaks

I wrap my canvas arms around you,
perhaps a little too tightly.
You stop struggling, your breathing quiets.
Inside my narrow kimono-like sleeves
your arms are nicely crossed and contained.
I hug your chest and shoulders and imagine you
in a coffin lined with red satin, a perfect
white camellia covering each eyelid.
I'm kind. I don't let them employ the crotch strap.
You walk freely around the grounds.
Although I never want to let you go,
don't they wrest me from you;
and doesn't the blood always rush back into your hands?
You know the routine. They will release you,
give you a spoon. You'll eat porridge.

BLACK BOX

Found Poem—taken from the testimony of Abu Zubaydah.

Two black boxes were brought into the room outside my cell. One was tall, slightly higher than me and narrow. The other was shorter. I was taken out of my cell. The interrogators wrapped a towel around my neck, used it to swing me around and smash me against the hard walls of the room. I was repeatedly slapped in the face. Shackled, the pushing and pulling pulled painfully on my ankles.

After the beating, I was placed in the small box. They put a cover to cut out all light and restricted my air supply. It was not high enough for me to sit up, I had to crouch down which was extremely difficult because of my wounds. The wounds in my legs started to open and bleed. I don't know how long I remained in the small box. I think I slept or fainted.

I was then dragged, unable to walk properly and put on a hospital bed and strapped down very tightly with belts. A black cloth was placed over my face. The interrogators poured mineral water on the cloth, so I could not breathe. After a few minutes the cloth was removed and the bed was rotated to an upright position. The pressure of the straps on my wounds were very painful. I vomited. I struggled against the straps, trying to breathe, but it was hopeless. I thought I was going to die. I lost control of my urine. I still lose control of my urine when I'm under stress.

Dr. Henry Anonymous Speaks at the 1972 APA Convention

The panel "Psychiatry: Friend or Foe of the Homosexual?" had a gay astronomer
and a lesbian activist. There was no psychiatrist, so one was recruited. In the DSMII
queerness was labeled a "disturbance of sexual orientation."

I am a homosexual.
I am a psychiatrist.

I'm not using my name.
I'm donning this ridiculous mask,
a baggy tuxedo, a bow tie,
a wig of wild curly hair,
to retain my current position.
Since Tricky Dick is still president,
it wasn't hard to find an easy-to-alter
Nixon mask in a joke shop.

We homosexual psychiatrists must deal
with what I call Negro syndromes.
We must know our place and be more 'healthy'
than our heterosexual counterparts.
When your fellow professionals denigrate
'the faggots,' . . . don't just stand by idly.

I've always been theatrical or flamboyant.
That's what I was called at my last position
when they fired me. I've been known
to wear wild patterned dashikis and bring
a room to order by ringing a cowbell.

So here I am, facing you,
speaking into a microphone
that warps my voice—
beseeching you to see this psychiatrist
not as a pervert, but merely a person
who prefers male partners to the female sex.

I'm wearing a mask,
but the one I always wear
doesn't peel off.

PRAYER OF A PEDOPHILE

I tried everything:
paid to talk to people about my uncle
who pulled me onto his lap; prayed to sky's
dark clouds; made myself a speck,
a slab of concrete, a body without a penis
or a mind, hoarded pills, ropes, pistols and knives,
which I'm too weak to use,

but I just read in a book, that some would call holy,
that I can be healed, and will no longer prey
on young boys. Now
I'm on a mission for redemption
with a new name, "sinner," and a recipe:

> *Two pure white doves*
> *cedarwood*
> *crimson yarn*
> *hyssop*
>
> *Set free one bird, behead the other*
> (A machete is suggested)
>
> *Smear blood on my right earlobe*
> *right thumb and toe of right foot*
> *Shave off all hair including eyebrows*
> *Immerse in a lake or pond*

Please, let me wake up tomorrow bright and early....
Perhaps finally, I won't be a roach
crawling under a table,
and will claim a seat.

Not sure where to find hyssop,
maybe dried mint will do.

NIGHTMARE, RECURRENT

I observe myself as if through a telescope.
Wearing a hospital gown tied in back,
sitting in a recovery room wallpapered
with pink hearts in a city I don't recognize.

The surgeons say they'll fix me right up,
cut out the video tape in my brain
of his pushing into me against the sink,
of his hands on my bare ankles
when I try to run.

How could a cousin make me so disgusting?
Something bad has to happen to him.
I don't care what. I just want my asshole
to be mine again.

It looks like all my stuff's here:
clothes, shoes, keys, coins, wallet, paperback
and a kiwi, a fruit I don't eat.

My boxers are on; each piece of clothing—
t-shirt, red flannel shirt, torn jeans, socks, hoodie,
Timbers cap, high tops, but I'm never ready
to walk through the automatic doors.

They lie, say I'm free to go.
But he is still inside me,
watching me whimper.

I sling my backpack over my shoulder,
plant my hands in my front pockets,
play with pennies, lint and the lanyard
I lost in sleepaway camp.

That's what I do, white knuckle it.
But I'll always be small. Him,
humongous.

SIM CARD SELLER

Once I was a goddess.
On my forehead I wore thick black make-up
of an open winged crow, red brocaded saris,
multiple strands of copper and gold necklaces,
heavy bangles circled my thin arms.

I was divine—the incarnation of Durga.
Decapitated buffaloes lying in pools of blood,
men whirling wearing ferocious fang masks
and tentacles of red hair would not frighten me.

I had all the perfections, so I was told: a moist tongue,
the thighs of a deer, the croon of a sparrow,
and like a conch-shell I held sacred water
as om vibrated through my marrow.
Everybody would bow before me,
their heads touching my perfumed toes.

Now I sell SIM cards to tourists who text
their heroics trekking Mother Annapurna.
I knew the palanquin would soon parade
the next Kumari through the streets.

I didn't act holy when I found blood on my panties,
I hid them beneath silk bedclothes
and strung marigolds.

SKIN

A black woman loans me her skin.
It doesn't fit like a bodystocking
or wetsuit. It becomes mine,
sepia and smooth.

I notice a puncture
on the left side of my torso.
There is blood. My thumb
fits in the slit and finds muscle.

The Band-Aids are the wrong color
and too small.

I must do something:

smash the leg irons,
shoot the master,
cut down the lynching tree.

Now the woman is in the hallway
wearing her skin. She says,
don't worry yourself, you
got your own: inked numbers,
yellow star

always there;

this wound
is mine.

FIFTY-MINUTE HOUR

Pearls

Dr. Martin T. Orne was Anne Sexton's psychiatrist.

I wish I could have been with you
and Dr. Orne in his office, you both sucking
in cigarette smoke, letting it curl out
through your nostrils, when you said,

I want to be the child not the mother.
It should be innate, why have I failed so miserably?

My words on paper spark, don't you think??

You thought writing might be good for me.
These runes are really yours too.

I would have seen you twist
the string of pearls around your neck
until it burst open, pearls cascading.

One by one, I would have picked them up,
to place them in your cupped hands—
all that milky light,

and say, "Your poems are your pearls,
yours alone."

THE FIRST THERAPIST

for Lenore Hecht

Her office was on West End Avenue.
There were paintings that looked like Pollack's
and Krasner's, jazzy and flung.

She wore a caftan patterned
with vertical ovals looped together, cuffed
with silver trim. Although old enough to be my mother,
no worry lines around her eyes. In the distance
the sepia Hudson River wasn't churning.

The world was a giant fist
blocking my vision,
a huge blackberry smear, with no
lighthouses or goldfinches. I told her,
All I want to do is sleep.

Being an only child,
I had to try this or remain stuck—
my mother cursing my father,
Go back to the nuthouse,
encasing me like a second skin.

Those weekly 50 minutes were my sanctuary,
my shoes off, my arms around my knees,
I sunk into cushions stitched with tiny mirrors,
muscles in my face unclenched,
and in my dreams sunflowers dwarfed
barbed wire fences.

She invited me to call her by her first name,
Lenore, and one exquisite time,
rocking me in her wide lap, Lenore
broke through the tradition's fourth wall
of no touch, as I laughed and tears
ran down my face, she assured me,
your life will be different
from those who birthed you.

WIND FREEZES TREES IN TORTURED POSITIONS

Esalen, Big Sur, 1980

She imagines mind crouching on one folding chair
heart enthroned in the other,
as she moves back and forth
between the two
mind saying, *don't*
heart saying, *do*
encounter yet another man

But this one, like her father
will not accept her.
This man will say, *You're too thin
your breasts too small*

THE UNSPOKEN

When I was still assigned clients
I read your chart:
>   *he stopped eating or bathing, defecated*
>   *in a jar, wouldn't leave brother's basement—*
>   *arrived via stretcher.*

Now, we meet once a week in my office.

I imagine your subsidized studio,
the ancient PC Voc. Rehab gave you
dominating the room, a sleep sofa
which grinds when you push it closed,
where you lie down alone.

For ten years you have come to me.

You don't know that I live with my lover
and that we bought a home. You
will never see our view
facing three mountains.

Alone together,
we face each other.
You have your place,
I have mine.

Others also visit. I know
you don't like to think of them.

Your anhedonia lifts a little.
You hold a job precariously
like a seal balancing a ball on his nose.

Your boss gives you a new laptop.
You crawl into the World Wide Web
and email no one
unless they email you.

I see you more often
than many of my friends.

In last week's session
the unimaginable happens:

you open your mouth—
a cry escapes,
a cross between a chuckle and choking,
tears sneak down your cheeks,
like drizzle in a sky where it never rains,

and you say, *does anyone care
if I live or die?*

I look directly into your wet eyes,
and think:

I know…
you love me,
I know.

Interviewing a New Therapist

I don't really know what I'm saying,
but I'll call it "empathetic linguistics."

When I say my mind freezes,
a therapist should be curious:

> *How does it feel to have a mind like that?*
> *How does it feel really?* A therapist might say,
> *It must be very frustrating when your mind screeches to a halt.*

I need to be understood:

Let's say I was molested by a tree.
It doesn't matter that trees are incapable of such things,
or that I have a fear of raindrops.
The worst thing you can do is respond, *rain isn't harmful,*
you go out in the rain all the time, in fact
you just came in from the rain. Sorry,
that negation of my feelings actually damages me.

I need compassion for the pain underneath,
so the memories of the original fucked-up things
done to me can emerge,
and I might heal.

Since my current therapist has no fucking clue,
I'll continue to cancel.

CONFIDENTIALITY

You carry their angst with you—
a basket filled with quivering raw eggs.
Clients must never know your fear of cracking.
You must embody what they barely tell themselves:

they are the man who shaves the right side of his face first,
instead of the left (for him that's the improper order),
and must scrape the left side again until it bleeds;

the woman who cries diabetes makes her husband slur
and unsteady as a drunk,
but refuses to be his nursemaid;

the young man who says he "understands"
why his girlfriend likes girls, so does he,
but since the threesome, he fears
she might really like girls more;

the wife of the sex-addict who hates
all the women in his computer,
and the whores, not virtual, and prays
her breast implants will win him back;

the senior who finally accepts his marriage is over,
although he rescued his much younger
wife from a cult, and now believes
he was no hero, just another master;

The mother who doesn't want her college age son
to move back if he smokes pot. This week, no talk
of her alcoholic paramour, "who has got to go."

Today, one exits, one walks in. The 2 o'clock
will never know the grief of the client before her,
whose twin embryos clotted out of her body,

and the 1 o'clock won't feel even worse, not knowing
that the 2 o'clock, who never wanted children, is elated
since her abortion went without a hitch.

For you, it's like holding a dragonfly by its wings
trying not to tear them off.

To Inhabit the Body

You tell me that as soon as those protrusions
sprouted, you knew they didn't belong.
They felt alien, you say,
as the frilly pastel undies
your mother made you wear.

Grown, your body becomes your canvas.
You are sleeved-up with blue snakes coiling
your arms, their tongues darting out
underneath your chin.

You understand it is different for me,
that I don't want a permanent
testament to anyone inked in my skin,
and that when my chest was renamed breasts,
I welcomed those modest orbs.

You tell me that no one will ever talk at your tits again.
We both agree that's a perk for you, and that jerks
ogling me is my burden for liking mine;

and you will awaken from surgery
relieved that underneath your bandages
your chest is flat like a door
which opens into a garden
where you find yourself inhabiting
the body you were meant to wear.

COUPLE COUNSELING

In the first session I always ask what is your hope for couple counseling? He says he is ready to put his marbles on the table. A few opaque ones slyly slip out. Hers flash primary colors and could fill buckets. She is willing to do whatever. The baby Is due in a month. He says there is the age difference. Now his marbles feel slightly rubbery and you can almost taste his fear. She says her father died young. She has always liked older men. Her marbles are becoming the size of robin's eggs shaped like tears. And there is the small matter of living in different countries and dreaming in disparate languages. He wants someone he can wake up with every day. She says all their separations make sex phenomenal. He doesn't disagree. Her marbles are falling onto the floor in clumps, as his re-harden into formation, the shape of a triangle for billiard balls. He is not willing to stop seeing the woman he met online. She holds her belly, marbles crack open, blood seeps out.

Dream Session, Client I

The panes in my apartment are small, don't open,
and there is a refrigerator with a cubbyhole
wide enough for the DSM and a spigot for tears.

You find the matzo and the jar of peanut butter,
help yourself, and say, *You probably have
another favorite client now.*

"I spy you floating around outside my office suite.
You never wear muumuus. Stop it, stop
knocking on every door but mine.
After so many years together you owe me
a finale and applause, but instead you jump ship."

You just couldn't, you say. *Sorry.
Please accept this dream good-bye.
With you I almost erased my mother.
If I ever turn myself inside out again
it won't be with you.*

You rub the crumbs off your mouth:
*Who knows? Without you
I might do the same old same old,
pick up men whose fists shut me up
and force me to change locks.*

Dream Session, Client II

I walk down a spindly railed staircase
from my private life to an unfinished basement
crammed with giant white plastic bags
filled with client files.

You stand at the foot of the stairs:

> *This could be a one-shot deal.*
> *I thought I would show up*
> *for my regular appointment*
> *to see if you had filled it.*

> *My parents are almost eighty now,*
> *and I still don't love them. I acquiesced*
> *to be with them in London.*

> *At the Tower we watched the Beefeaters*
> *march stiffly into place.*
> *I couldn't wait to get away.*

I am dreaming, so I can self-disclose
visiting the Big Apple, and not telling my parents
I was down the street, and divulge

that although my mother said "that when you were young
you loved your father best," I don't remember
ever loving him.

REALITY TESTING

TASTERS

Hitler is a vegetarian.
You hold a crust in your cheek.

Daughters of the Deutschland
taste his food on bone china.

You gnaw on a potato peel.

A rose petal is a swastika
in the center of each plate.

You suck on a fingernail of schmaltz.

The girl with braids pulled tight against her skull
puts the tip of an asparagus spear in her mouth.

The water called soup won't stay down.

The one with skyless blue eyes swallows
creamy white cauliflower florets.
Will she keel over?

You palm a bit of turnip.
The Fuhrer doesn't butcher animals.

Another Fraulein licks a perfect red pepper.

There is room to lie on your side.
Your head won't lift up.
Your mouth is a pit.

Prayer of an Apotemnophile

Please...you must release me.

Although I have two eyes, two breasts and all the rest,
my legs below the knee are surplus baggage.
Without them my body is perfect,
made in your image.

Hear my pleas and make me whole.

Perhaps if toes could turn up like leprechaun shoes
I might feel differently. The Chinese bound
women's feet. They saw those tootsies
for the useless appendages they truly are.

I won't be an amputee, or labeled disabled.
They don't choose. I'll walk on my hands
twirl on a trapeze, hurl myself from rope to rope
and somersault holding on to ski poles.

Merciful God, help me find a surgeon.

I'll breeze around town in a shiny electric wheelchair,
show off my polished stumps. The curve
of my knees will be graceful as a swan's head,
smooth as snow globes with Xmas scenes.

Lord, take from me what is not of me.

If you don't, I will find a landmine to step on,
a mercenary delighted to sever
my calves from my thighs, tracks
where a train is coming to cleave
those extraneous extremities.

You wouldn't want your lamb
to take matters into her own hands.
Would you?

MISSING PERSON

Like a daddy long legs   I'll wash down the drain
Don't make me shower   I'm dressed and ready
Socks over socks   hide-holes of the one beneath   long johns
jeans with patches   terrycloth robe   puffy coat
feathers leaking out   Don't want to freeze sleeping outside
Don't want you to see my scrawny body either
You could corner me and know my name   My hair
hides itself under this cruddy woolen beanie   easy pull down
over my crumpled face   If I don't see you   you don't see me
Like somebody famous   my hair gives me strength
wraps around and around itself — a wound-up
extension cord   I went to the cops, said, I'm missing
can you find me? You think I'm funny   Don't even think
of yanking my dink off   My slick black shoe polish hair gate
will electrocute you

Now I Don't Ask

Munchausen by proxy syndrome (MBPS) involves the exaggeration or fabrication of symptoms by a primary caregiver.

Mommy says I get sick an awful lot. She takes care of me great. She tucks me in with my Barbies, Beanie Babies and my wood choo-choo train. I watch DVDs of Captain Kangaroo and Mr. Green Jeans, mommy's friends when she was little.

The wooden spoon with the hole in the end for the string stays on the hook when I'm sick. My behind doesn't sting then, and I don't have to play with Tommy, who is older than me, and always pulls down his pants.

I know how to make myself throw-up. I barf until there is nothing inside me, and #2 is water. We go to the emergency room so often everyone knows us. Mommy sounds smart talking to the doctors.

The man who mommy said is my daddy visited once. He threw her coffeepot, her favorite thing, (I loved the sound the perc made and how the brown water jumped inside the glass knob), out the window. Mommy fixed the window with cardboard and duck tape, then said, *Mommy's sick, going to lie down.* I wanted to play nurse, put a thermometer under her tongue, but she yelled, *Get away from me!*

Sometimes Mommy tells me to pee into a used-up peanut butter jar. She says, *Hospitals need samples.* Sometimes her bedroom door is open a crack. I see her with a sewing kit needle making skinny lines across her arms then squeezing the blood out, unscrewing the lid of a jar with my pee, and sticking a bloody finger inside. Yellow and red look so pretty together. Once in a loud voice I asked, *Why?* The big wooden spoon came off the hook.

PSYCHOSIS

Found Poem

The world was in Rembrandt colors, rich and darkly glowing. Miss Sharp, [the head nurse], never stood still. She was tall and thin and walked briskly. From a distance she looked like a devil and I was surprised to find how nice she was when I spoke to her. The lines in her face stuck out like big, skinny bones, but she wasn't sticky or pushy. I felt she wanted to help me. I felt bathed by colors of her skin and her bony lines made me feel alive. They were spikes and spurs to climb with. She was a mountain. She popped out of the picture. I remember the first moment I thought, Why she's a real person! It was the first time I saw someone who was not mainly a devil. For days I stole glimpses of her to check if it was really true.

FLORID

MOON

Why aren't you here yet
to glow tombstones
in the cemetery at dusk?

Finally.
I glue my eyes to your cool light
and gauzy shimmer,
until you do my bidding,
slinking down on the mowed grass

stretching full and wide, enveloping me
in your diaphanous globe body,
upward, we float.

But you will tire of me,
everyone does,
your silvery seam will rip open.
Inert as a grave marker,
I'll fall flat, back
to where death is.

TREE

You inch towards me,
with your shapely trunk,
full head of leaves and supple limbs.

You seduce me with your furrowed bark,
white and scaly with black frowns
and mascara-lidded eyes.
Your splinters are tongue kisses.

You make my body gossamer,
burrowing deep inside your hollow,
through inner bark and sapwood,
to heartwood, I'm alive here,

but someone will call my name,
tell me I'm sick again, and kidnap me
to a foreign place called home.

72" x 72"

for Agnes Martin

The voices were prohibitive—don't buy
land, no cats or dogs, nothing but canned
tomatoes, walnuts and hard cheese, but
they couldn't see the map, the gift of her
mind's eye—a square postage stamp-size
grid of lightly penciled slightly uneven
rectangles, and couldn't thwart the platting
from materializing on a gessoed stretched
canvas that would be propped up against
her studio wall. The boxes she ruled were
not padded cells for bodies of coiled black
lines, but hives of gold leaf and moving
clouds.

HER RORSCHACH

My wife asks so often, she's wearing me down.

I administered the Rorschach at Sisters of Mercy
so long ago, that the kids' pain, like a bullet
lodged in my brain, shouldn't
affect me anymore.

My wife has a great imagination.
She wants to take the Rorschach for fun.

I'll wipe the dust off the cardboard box of 10 "plates"—
Hermann Rorschach, *Psychodiagnostik / Psychodiagnostics*
on the cover, copyright 1921, renewed 1948.

The worst that ever happened to her
was that her father threatened to slap her, while
my kids' parents tied them to chairs
or beat them with gun butts.

I would say:
>   *These are inkblots. A lot of people see more than one thing.*
>   *I want you to tell me what you see.*

She'll see beings winged or horned
behemoths on springs in the fuzzy blobs, not
humanoids with bloody heads and bloody, oozing legs.

She'll see whiskered genies in profiles on molten roller skates,
not pink cheetahs forever crawling up a plastic bucket
and sliding down into yellow piss.

She'll see bunnies in tuxedos,
albumen egg heads sprouting yellow tails,
not hands pushing, a fight starting—
everything on fire.

My wife will have no diagnostic label attached to her.
She will not pray for a new foster home where abuse
might not be replicated.

I had it easy too. My father offered to pay me
100 bucks if I would not smoke.
He was too late, years before on my paper route
I was already dragging on those cancer sticks.

If I go through with it, and test her, she'll thank me
with a special cocktail. These days her pleasure
is something purplish and foamy.

TERMINATION

Moving

My head is leaden and my shoes stone.
I own two dwellings. One is lonely and empty.
Its fuchsia and Japanese maple cry.
The other barely knows me, toys with me,
and has hidden my fettling knife and writing book.

Once I could make letters, few or many,
into words angels would whisper,
but now, I can only muster,
"wastepaper basket," "toilet roll."

I ride up and down with the weary
whose houses also left them.
I know the key is on the 13th floor,
but it's missing from the panel of buttons
and I have no magic to get me there.

Before, my divan knew solitude.

I recline into her armless back.
The bridge between my waning life, and
my inchoate one is a burnt offering.

Outside the window ash falls.

Toxic

Come to bed.
Not if you're going to bite my head off.

Just stop lying.
You're the liar.

You weren't with Skye and her friend.
You purposely left your cell at home.

You don't trust me? I don't trust you either.
You never do anything you say you're gonna do.

Didn't I fix the pilot light?
How many months after you said you would?

You pile the dishes in the sink, until we have to use paper plates.
At least I can cook something besides grilled cheese.

You're on a roll. You used to love me inside you.
Now you won't even let me brush a crumb off your face.

I don't want you near me after…
Remember, you said 'a rhino is more sexy.'

I know my crying disgusts you.
Remember, I'm fucking pathetic.

If you grab my arm again, I'll call the cops.
If you grab my arm again, I'm outta here.

Couple counseling didn't work.
Duh. You wouldn't change.

I just wanted him to know it wasn't all me.
You just wanted him to side with you.

HUG-A-THUG

Psychiatric technician Harriet Krzykowski worked on the Psych Unit of Dade Correctional Institution.

My patients voices tell them they are too stupid to hang themselves,
a bat pleads with one to teach him to fly,
another rips up his bible looking for God,
everyone stands motionless
in the middle of their cells when they hear birdsong.

Water coming out of the faucet in the breakroom scalds.
When I want it less hot, I'm scolded, *Mrs. Hug-A-Thug,*
what's your problem?

The guys are psychotic, right, so of course
they make things up, but not everything. They report
empty trays with no lunch shoved into solitary, whisper
to me that guards taunt, *Go kill yourself—*
no one will miss you.

One bangs and bangs his foodless tray against metal bars
until they take even that away.

"Put him in the shower" means
at temperatures that brew tea or make ramen.

A psycho shits in his cell, refuses
to clean it up, and is put in the shower.
When the corpse is touched, the skin falls off.

Again, I'm Going through Rooms

for Margarita Donnelly

I

I drift through railroad flat rooms—
a bedroom with wainscoting,
a silent parlour, into a kitchen,
opened presents, torn wrapping paper
and babies on the floor.
People with lines in their faces
sit on chairs missing spindles. They joke
and drink out of cracked blue bowls.
They don't sense me already moving into the future.
They are too happy.

II

They left these low-ceilinged rooms
in a hurry. Dresser drawers are slowly closing.
A soft-boiled egg is still in its porcelain cradle.
In the hall closet I find a fedora and bury
my nose in a mink stole on its wire skeleton.
I look for something handwritten.
There is no note.

III

These rooms, I know.
I have slept in long johns and wool socks
in the bed above her bed. I am cold.
I go into the room that is no longer hers,
she who tasted the Spanish tamarind
and the soursop in her sleep.
I pull back the covers, and cup my hands
over the sag in the middle.

Moonlight

This time, the truck, the dirt road,
the field is in Srebrenica.

He is packed in a battered flatbed
with other men,
old, young,
whimpering in fear.

The truck lurches a few kilometers
down a back road.
Five hauled out. Five shots.
A few more kilometers,
four dragged out. Four shots.

Again, the truck comes to a halt.
A boot on his rump pushes him out.

His wrists tied,
he lies face down,
hears gunfire,
tastes blood, perhaps his own.

Crabgrass marks the man's face.
His nostrils are forgetting
how to take in air.

The moon is full.
In all directions it stares
at human beings past sorrow,
and now this man,
the weight of his silenced body
pressing into the unfurrowed field.

Paying Homage

We all used to robotrip cough syrup and retch together, but if me and Suzie chugged a bottle, she upended two. She wasn't like the rest of us. I liked seeing myself on top of a church steeple, a puffy cloud like a hat on my head. She felt an iceberg stabbing her, her hands frozen to its sides.

Going to the creek to skinny-dip she would find a slab of granite, rub the sole of her foot along its razor edge, when blood started gushing her laughter would explode. Our bandages were extra t-shirts.

Once I took her to the ER. I'm not her mother or her sister, or anyone like that. I stayed in the waiting room and punched candy out of a vending machine. Midol more than took away our cramps, and everything made us crack up, but she ate those pills like tic tacs. They put a tube down her stomach and a big syringe sucked them out, *like they were diamonds*, she snarled. For her, it was no big deal.

Soon hot sauce wasn't hot enough for us. We needed to feel like we were manufacturing it ourselves and lava was erupting out of our veins. That's when I started carrying around Narcan. If someone took too much Vikes or Oxy and fingertips and lips turned purple, and they were gasping for breath or not waking up when I slapped them, I would push the nasal spray nozzle right in their nose. In no time they would come back to life. Everyone else thought I was Mother Teresa or something, but she would hiss at me, I *almost made a home run this time. Even my parents want to put me out of my misery. They're in my head telling me 'you're better off dead.'*

I'll never know. She wasn't like the rest of us. She wanted to die. We just wanted to get high. Hope she felt she was the sharpest knife in the nuthouse drawer. The morons were supposed to issue her a suicide blanket, paper scrubs and keep the bathroom stalls locked, instead they gave her a terrycloth robe with a long sash.

SUICIDE FOREST

Ubasute, (Japanese) means abandoning an old woman.

After finding me wandering
without a blouse,
my son became infuriated.

Once upon a time he would have carried me
on his back into the Sea of Trees,
but now he grabs my wrist to bruise;

gnarled and twisted silver-fir limbs embrace
each other so tightly wind has no room to gust;
my little wind catches in the throat.

Once escorts snapped twigs to find their way out;
my son winds blue tape between trees
so dense no sky or Fuji-san.

We push past cypress and hemlock
where nooses hang, t-shirts hug trunks,
knives stab bark, torn typed notes decompose.

My son marches.
I pant and stumble, his hand a vise.
I will remember his face,
the mole beneath his left nostril.

I pry off his fingers.

Until I cannot, I'll forage.

Ribbons of blue tape
will return him to the living.

FACING SUICIDE BRIDGE

It takes three seconds to fall twelve stories.

My window faces a mountain that looks like a cupcake,
a pink building with a flattened face
and the bridge of despair.

I should move.

I feel her out there standing
on one of its cement benches
ready to dive.

Their pain is a crevasse so vast
no one can pull them out; they have become
beings beyond caring about the anguish
their broken bodies will bring.

Her hoodie billows out as she drops.
She crashes on the tracks, her head tucked in her arm.
Blood seeps from her nostrils.

I want the bodies to stop falling.
I call 911 always too late.

Everyone dies. At least these bridge walkers
have chosen when and where.

The sound of a person hitting the ground
from a great height is hard to describe.
It is sort of like slamming
your hand down with full force
on a table. It will ache for days.

In The Snooker Room

Prince Dipendra murdered his parents, the King and Queen of Nepal and eight other members of the Royal family. Devyani Rana was the woman he wished to marry.

Those few minutes are etched in my brain, as if I scratched
them into my arms, recut them with a razor blade
before the wounds could heal.

Now, except when I lie down and guilt dreams don't insinuate,
sleeping or waking are no different.

> *in the snooker room he wears black army boots*
> *a camouflage jacket and vest drunk and high*
> *he staggers around holding a sub-machine gun*
> *and an assault rifle*

If I was allowed into the Royal Palace
I could have prevented it.
We were forced to sneak around.
I had too much Indian blood. *Ranas* serve royals.
They don't marry would be kings.

> *screaming   acrid smell of gun powder*
> *people falling   blood oozing   smatterings of brain tissue*
> *bits of glass bangles   fragments of jaws*

I would have taken his face in my hands, and said, *I love you,*
I will always love you, put those weapons down, darling,
they are not toys.

Dipendra would have acquiesced. All that self-loathing
would have slid off his shoulders, as we wept,
he would have covered my face with kisses.

ITALIAN PLUMS

for Sarah Lantz

We climb up lichen-encrusted limbs,
to pluck purple-black fruit,
protected with white powder
that hides their sheen.

We are inundated with plums,
burdened by bounty.

Why do we merit
this small happiness:
plums boiling down in the big stainless
steel pot, mason jars brimming with jam,
brown paper bags bulging
with enough for everyone.

If only this plethora of plums could bring you back,
but their days are even shorter than yours.
They have burst their skins
and are staining pavement.

You were alive, but are no longer,
and will not savor the juice
of even one small plum.

SHELLEY'S HEART

We talk how easy it is
to jump holding hands,
to die at the same moment,
sprint over the half-window of our high-rise downtown,
crumple on the ground, our eyes open.

Percy Shelley's fragile craft capsized near Livorno.
His heart in a "furnace of iron" refused to burn.
Mary wrapped her beloved's broken pump
in a page of his elegy to Keats.

They were together for ten years.
We have more than doubled that.

If you are taken from me I won't hold your heart
in my cupped hands, swaddled in your words:
Go deeper, equanimity is not the goal.

I caress your Buddha earlobes,
pinch your ass shapeless inside your torn jeans,
hear your voice resonant and sure as a singing bowl,

and in bed, you on your back, my side body and neck
nest into you, as if we would always
fit that way.

Notes

Unsanctioned: Inmates wrote for *The Opal: A Monthly Periodical*, New York State Lunatic Asylum, Utica, 1851 - 1860. Dr. John P. Gray was the superintendent.

The Majesty of Mania: Clifford Whittingham Beers was institutionalized in private and public mental hospitals from 1900 - 1903. He went on to revolutionize the care and treatment of the mentally ill.

Intake at the Canton Asylum for Insane Indians: The Canton Asylum for Insane Indians, AKA Hiawatha Insane Asylum in South Dakota existed from 1898 - 1934. It was the only mental institution in the US created exclusively for one minority group.

American History: Vaishno Das Bagai died March 17, 1928.

Vapor: Marcy Border was photographed by Stan Honda. She recovered from substance addiction in 2011, and died of stomach cancer four years later at the age of forty-two.

Song of A Rental Sister: "Rental Sisters" are employed to help mostly young men, hikkomori, to leave their homes and return to normal society. Hikkomori is the name for the condition, and for the individual(s) who has the condition. About one in sixty Japanese age 15 - 64 identify as hikkomori.

Exposure, 1856: Research for this poem was taken from *The Face of Madness: Huge W. Diamond and the Origin of Psychiatric Photography* edited by Sander L. Gilman, (Citadel Press, 1977). John Conolly, (1794 - 1866), considered a leading British psychiatrist of the period, wrote case studies about patients Diamond photographed at the Surrey County Lunatic Asylum. Conolly's lecture is imagined.

Like Coring An Apple: António Egaz Moniz developed the prefrontal lobotomy for which he received a Nobel Prize in 1949. He never actually performed the surgery. In 1935, Pedro Almeida Lima under Moniz's supervision, performed the first psychosurgery.

She Was A Kennedy: Rosemary Kennedy received a lobotomy in 1941, at the age of 23. Much of the research for this poem was taken from *Rosemary: The Hidden Sister* by Kate Clifford Larsen, particularly, pg.75, (Mariner Books, 2015). The "letters" are imagined.

Black Box: Taken from Abu Zubaydah's testimony to the International Committee of the Red Cross. He was the first person subjected to the CIA's torture program designed and implemented by psychologists James Mitchell and Bruce Jessen. Abu Zubaydah is still housed at Guantanamo Bay.

Dr. "Henry Anonymous" Speaks at the 1972 APA Convention: Dr. John E. Fryer was "Dr. Anonymous." His speech has been cited as a key factor in the decision to de-list homosexuality as a mental illness from the APA's *Diagnostic and Statistical Manual of Mental Disorders*. The words in italics are taken directly from his speech. Today, comparing the homophobia Fryer experienced to "the Negro syndrome" would be unacceptable.

SIM Card Seller: Kumari, or Living Goddess is the Nepalese tradition of worshipping prepubescent girls as manifestations of divine female energy.

Prayer Of An Apotemnophile: Apotemnophilia is an overwhelming or obsessive desire to have one or more healthy body parts, especially a limb, removed by amputation.

The found poem **Psychosis** was taken from the patient "Carl's," (a pseudonym) words in *The Psychotic Core* by Michael Eigen, Ph.D., pg. 140-141, (Jason Aronson, Inc. 1986).

Florid was inspired by Michael Eigen's descriptions of two of "Carl's" psychotic periods; *The Psychotic Core*.

72" x 72": Abstract painter, Agnes Martin (1922 - 2004) was diagnosed with paranoid schizophrenia.

Her Rorschach: In 1921, Hermann Rorschach created the inkblot test, a psychological test in which subjects' perceptions of inkblots are recorded and then analyzed.

Hug-A-Thug: Was inspired by the article "Madness," by Eyal Press, *The New Yorker*, April 25, 2016.

Facing Suicide Bridge: The actual name for this Portland, Oregon bridge is Vista Bridge. It earned its nickname because from 2004 - 2011, thirteen people died jumping off.

In The Snooker Room: Dipendra Bir Bikram Shah Dev telephoned Devyani Rana prior to his rampage on June 1, 2001. She has never expressed publicly what she knew.

ACKNOWLEDGMENTS

I want to express my gratitude to Patricia Bollin for her critical acumen as an early reader of this manuscript, also to Susan Russell who read it at a later stage, and to members of my two critique groups, The Odds and the Moonlit Poetry Caravan, who reviewed most of these poems. Their critique was invaluable. I especially want to thank my friend and sister poet Frances Payne Adler, whose support helped me get this work into the world.

~

Grateful acknowledgment to the editors of the following journals and anthologies, in which poems were published, republished or forthcoming, (some in different versions):

Asylum, The Radical Mental Health Magazine: "Admission Criteria For Oregon State Insane Asylum, 1906"

Bellevue Literary Review: "The Bodies Are Messages"

Beltway Quarterly Review: "In The Snooker Room;" "Wind Freezes Trees In Tortured Positions"

Calyx: A Journal of Art & Literature by Women: "Italian Plums;" "Again, I'm Going Through Rooms"

Cirque: A Literary Journal for the North Pacific Rim: "There Are Countries"

The Citron Review: "Shelley's Heart"

Fireweed: "The Unspoken"

Gyroscope Review: "Moving"

Harpur Palate: "Love"

International Psychoanalysis: "Couple Counseling;" "To Inhabit the Body;" "Tiny Monuments"

Minyan: "Florid"

Mudfish: "Ugly;" "Again, I'm Going Through Rooms"

Naugatuck River Review: "Prayer Of A Sleep Eater"

Passager: "Iron Lung," Honorable Mention, *Passager's* 2022 Poetry Contest

Poetica Magazine: "Tasters"

Poet Lore: "Moonlight;" "Like Coring An Apple;" "Suicide Forest"

Radical Teacher: "Skin;" "Dr. Henry Anonymous Speaks At The 1972 APA Convention;" "Unsanctioned"

Salmagundi: "The Tub Seduction;" "Nightmare, Recurrent"

The Journal of Psychohistory: "Yellow Halo"

Tikkun: "American History," also read by the poet in the inaugural podcast, *Voices of Tikkun*

VoiceCatcher: "Tiny Monuments;" "To Inhabit the Body"

Windfall: "Facing Suicide Bridge"

≈

"Confidentiality;" "Dream Session, Client I;" "Dream Session Client, II;" "Pearls" are forthcoming in *The Work Anthology*, Unleash Press.

"Admission Criteria For Oregon State Insane Asylum, 1906" will be republished as a proem in Matthew Smith's forthcoming book, *The First Resort: The History of Social Psychiatry in the United States*, Columbia University Press.

"The Majesty of Mania" was commended in the 2022 Fellowship of Postgraduate Medicine-Hippocrates Health Professional Prize for Poetry and Medicine and will be published in the *Hippocrates Awards Anthology*, (Hippocrates Initiative, UK, 2022).

"I" was published and "Tiny Monuments" was republished in *A Tapestry of Voices: An East Tennessee Anthology*, (Knoxville Writers' Guild Press, 2011).

"Life Line" and "The First Therapist," *Voices Israel Anthology*, (Voices Israel Group of Poets in English, 2021)

Molly Mayo's song "Archipelago" was taken from "Tiny Monuments" with some alterations.

ABOUT THE AUTHOR

Willa Schneberg is a poet, ceramic sculptor, interdisciplinary artist, essayist, curator and a Licensed Clinical Social Worker, (LCSW) in private practice. She is the author of five prior collections, including *In the Margins of the World*, *Storytelling in Cambodia*, and *The Books of Esther*, a letterpress chapbook produced in conjunction with the eponymous interdisciplinary exhibit, which was on view at the Oregon Jewish Museum and Center for Holocaust Education (OJMCHE). *Storytelling in Cambodia* was inspired by her time working for the United Nations Transitional Authority in Cambodia.

Among the honors she has received are the Oregon Book Award in Poetry, the Barbara Deming Memorial Fund Award, Second Place in the Allen Ginsberg Poetry Awards, inclusion in *The Year's Best Fantasy and Horror Nineteenth Collection*, two fellowships in Poetry from Literary Arts, Inc., residencies at Yaddo, MacDowell and Kathmandu, Nepal, and poems on the Writer's Almanac. Her poetry has been translated into Hebrew, Arabic, Nepali and Korean.